When My Heart Sings

Brenda Carroll Jarvis

Golden Street Ministries

Published by:

Golden Street Ministries LLC

Box 2

Farmdale, OH 44417

CONTENTS

INTRODUCTION

When I was young, I enjoyed writing down my thoughts. It helped to express what was happening within me. As life moved forward, with marriage, young children, jobs and time on the mission field, I didn't seem to find the time for writing.

After a broken marriage, as I struggled with my emotions, financial problems and social changes, my desire to write came back to me. I found that writing helped to bring healing and clarity of my thoughts. The Holy Spirit enlightened me with truth that brought peace to my heart.

Within these pages is a compilation of writings from 2010, when I began to write again. Since then, I have authored poems, essays, stories, books, and even song lyrics!

I pray some of these poems and other writings will touch your heart in a special way.

DEDICATION

This book is first dedicated to my Lord and Savior, who helped me to put words together and to write to express what was in my heart.

Then to the man that the Lord put in my life, Charles. He helped to bring beauty back to my life.

A GIFT OF SUNRISE

Each day's sunrise is a heavenly gift,

and as the days quickly became years,

then the years transformed into a lifetime,

then the lifetime became

a legacy for our family.

May your every day

be filled with the presence of God

THE CLOCK

I hear, the sound of the clock with its loud chime,

It orders our movements announcing the time.

Time to plan, time to go, time to come, time to meet,

Time to travel, time to work, time to play, time to eat.

Time moves too quickly when life's pace is fast,

Time drags on so slowly when all that's left has passed.

Time demands, as it crowds its way into our dreams,

With each tick, each movement of the clock, it screams.

Time is a bully; it steals our freedom and the joys of life,

It tries to grip us to have us doubt, causing more strife.

Time taunts, "It's too late, there is no more time", is its chant,

In a moment of despair, when I think it is over, I say, "I just can't."

A truth bursts into my weary heart, a word, a promise so true,

God's hands hold time, He knows each moment I go through.

"He has made everything beautiful in its time." His word states,

It is God that determines the plans, the timing, and the dates.

He reminds us to follow Him, let Him make our plan each day,

God knows the beginning from the end, He will show the way.

So now whenever the chime of the clock will sound,

I am free from the grip that time had me bound.

I am not trapped by time, nor a time-seeker,

My God, my father, He is the timekeeper.

But about that day or hour no one knows,

not even the angels in heaven, nor the Son,

but only the Father.

Matthew 24:36 NIV

Dawn's Promise

As the Dawn breaks through the sky,

The radiant glow pushes back the night.

The dark must give way to the brightness of the Dawn.

The cold of the night begins to fade to the warmth of the light.

As the Dawn begins to cast its glow on all things,

The trees begin to blush with the rising Dawn,

The flowers turn to the Dawn's radiance.

The birds come from their hiding places for the warmth it brings.

Each Dawn brings renewed strength,

For those who seek light

New hope and fresh vigor come with each Dawn.

Listen to the songs of the birds as they warm in the glow.

It fills the air with a melody of God's provision for each day.

The Dawn tells us that the night has its boundaries.

The coldness is held to a limit,

The emptiness of the night is bound by an unseen power.

The darkness must yield to the light of the Dawn.

Today is a new Dawn in our lives.

The Dawn breaks through our broken hearts,

It thaws the cold that the long night had brought.

No longer will the darkness hinder the journey,

The loneliness gives way to the warmth of the light,

The emptiness fades with renewed hope and purpose.

The Dawn stirs our spirit to the rebirth of our expectations.

The Dawn produces faith in the provision of our Father,

For our every need, hope and desire.

The Dawn teaches us to endure the night,

And then we rejoice in the Dawn.

The path of the righteous is like the first gleam of dawn,

shining ever brighter till the full light of day.

Proverbs 4:18

AN ENEMY LURKS NEARBY

There is an enemy that is lurking nearby,

It has a disguise of thoughts noble and high.

It is often handed down from another generation,

It becomes the building bricks of life's foundation.

It's hatred, the enemy to life and liberty,

It brings its gift of emptiness and misery.

Hatred can begin when one is young or old,

It creeps in secretly, quietly to take hold.

It looks for hearts that are bitter and hurt,

Those pains so deep get twisted, then used to convert.

Soon the soul fills with bitterness, conflict, and spite,

Requires energy, resentment, and always ready to fight.

The result is a churning of anger and rage,

Destruction of lives and beyond, who can gauge?

The eyes become like broken windows of the soul,

Vision is distorted increasing its planned control.

Hatred alters the vision of how life is seen,

It changes the understanding in every scene.

Hatred comes to steal, destroy, and divide,

It forces everyone, everywhere to choose a side.

Hatred takes and takes, never to be satisfied,

It replaces something pure for defiled.

Hatred is thirsty and hungers for more,

It creates anger then war, to settle the score.

Hatred can steal laughter from the merry heart,

It is a poison that contaminates from the start.

Hatred demands more, invading the homes,

It seeks new places to conquer as it roams.

Hatred brings division brother from brother,

Forgetting the bond of having the same mother.

When hatred moves in, whether in home or heart,

The damage does its work, tearing things apart.

Hatred does not build up, it only tears down,

It tramples lives, hopes, and dreams of all around.

Hatred seems too powerful to defeat, you might say,

There is only one solution, there is only one way.

Hatred can be destroyed at the only fount divine,

To be washed and transformed in Jesus' bloodline.

God's grace and mercy are the antidotes for hatred,

To live knowing and loving that each life is sacred.

Forgiveness begins the healing process,

Freedom from the weight, chaos and mess.

The power of God's love will renew and restore,

Jesus tells us that, He knocks on each heart's door.

Waiting for the opening, for new life's foundation,

He says that with Him, we are a new creation.

Hate will no long rule in a heart transformed by the cross,

Sharing God's love, so that not one soul be lost.

One by one each heart needs the purest love shared,

By our lives, words and actions, God's message is declared.

Be sober, be vigilant;
because your adversary the devil,
as a roaring lion, walketh about,
seeking whom he may devour.

1 Peter 5:8 KJV

WEARY FEET

As He traveled each day, on roads dusty, hot and long,
Often weary and tired from teaching the throng.
At times looking for a moment of rest, to pray,
Obeying his Father's commands never to sway.

Lying on the grass watching the splendor of the night,
How the countless stars were placed to the left and right.
The glow of the reflecting light of the midnight moon,
Knowing His divine destiny, His death was coming soon.

Another dawn and town, will these believe, will they hear?
He's the Messiah, they have waited for, year after year.
Coming as a babe to Bethlehem, a little-known town,
He had laid aside His throne and heavenly crown.

Angels' song filled the heavens to shepherds in a field,

They witnessed this babe, the promise of God revealed.

Kings came from afar, following a bright star.

Giving a box of gold, and costly spices in decorated jars.

Traveling through the land, healing the sick, raising the dead,

To some His miracles are hope, others a threat as the news spread.

His disciples talk with Him on other roads they traverse,

To announce redemption and freedom from the curse.

His feet are calloused, tired, dirty and so often sore,

Yet His heart of passion, for the lost, the message to restore.

The miles He journeyed on those roads, we do not know,

In parables, He speaks of lost coins and farmers who sow.

The cross comes closer as each day passes,

Is the message heard by anyone among the masses?

To know release from burdens, temptation and sin,

To tell of the grace, mercy, love and joy within.

I now understand the woman one night as she knelt so low,

Seeing the feet of her Savior, He freed her of debt and sorrow.

Her tears on his feet, she kissed them then dried with her hair,

The costly fragrant oil from her alabaster box she did not spare.

Her life transformed by His forgiveness, mercy and grace.

By His word all her sins were gone without a trace.

The beautiful, weary feet of the Savior, still bring good news,

Do you hear him calling? It is your decision, your time to choose.

How beautiful upon the mountains Are the feet of him who,

brings good news, who proclaims peace, who brings glad.

tidings of good things, who proclaims salvation, who,

says to Zion, "Your God reigns!"

ISAIAH 52:7 NKJV

HOLD MY HAND

Hold my hand as you travel, I hear my father say,

The steps are uncertain down the winding way.

The path leads to life's long-awaited dreams,

Many start the journey but lose their footing it seems.

My footsteps are guarded as I look for the way,

I dare not to hurry or to glance away.

I cautiously listen for my father's voice,

A seemingly easier path is not my choice.

I sense the firmness of his hand on mine,

I feel safe knowing this is His design.

Often I ask Him to question my pace,

My Father reminds me to stay steady. It is not a race.

The dreams that were planted in my heart long ago,

The desire and wishes I thought I would never know.

That force moves my feet further toward the goal,

And I know my Father guides me with complete control.

Hold my hand as you travel, I hear my Father say,

The steps are uncertain down the winding way.

Too easy to stumble and too quickly to fall,

If I turn a deaf ear to His loving call.

The way to the goal is not for the faint,

It is real wisdom to know restraint.

I ask my father "Where is the light?"

He tells me, "It does not come from eyes sight."

It's sensing His leading through his gentle touch,

It's to know His voice and His heart so much.

Each turn that is made down the dream pathway,

Is a silent conversation only true love will convey.

His hand steadies the stumble that threaten a fall,

His constant care for dangers great and small.

Help me each step to reach my heart's goal,

Without Him I am half not whole.

He smiles as I journey with my trust in his hand,

I know now my best is always His plan.

For I know the plans I have for you,

declares the LORD,

plans to prosper you and not to harm you,

plans to give you hope and a future.

Jeremiah 29:11 NIV

So, What Is New?

So, what is new? I was asked today,
I thought quickly about what to say.
Should I talk about an ache or pain?
Or maybe the coming storm and rain.

Do I mention the same old familiar talk?
Mimicking the sound of a parrot's squawk.
Should I just tell of the same ol' stuff,
Or just try to pretend to hide a bluff.

Should I say I have found a new hope?
I have a new life and a new way to cope!
What will be said when he hears?
Will he be happy or speak jeers?

So, what's new today? I want to shout,

I'm free, it is amazing, I have no doubt!

Let me tell you, my shame is gone,

I have new mercy each day, each dawn.

My shame, guilt, and sin is under the blood,

I am rescued and cleansed from death's mud.

I was ransomed, forgiven, my life's debt was paid,

From God's loving heart, redemption was made.

Hearts are hungry for this message of hope!

People are weary as they wander and grope.

Our message brings love, joy and light,

To restore and make whole is Jesus' delight.

So next time when someone asks, "What's new?"

Tell them, "Sit down, I have great news for you!"

For God so loved the world,

that he gave his only begotten Son,

that whosoever believeth in Him

should not perish, but have everlasting life.

John 3:16 KJV

WHAT I HEAR

Is what I hear reality or some strange illusion?

If the latter, may this not come to conclusion.

Shall I take the risk, do I open my eyes?

Do I turn my head upward to see the skies?

To see the dark clouds have faded,

And know the loneliness is abated.

If it be reality, these words are true,

Fall on my dry heart like morning dew.

Drops of purity touch what's forgotten,

No longer so dry but as soft as new cotton.

To revive in me the heart to thirst,

Allowing myself to be immersed.

To bring new life like the freshness of spring,

Forgetting winters passed – a new beginning.

The tone of His voice is balm to my soul.

Bringing new hope and desire that life stole.

The gentle expression of love so pure,

He reminds me, I am safe and secure.

The words conveyed are like a blanket wrapped round.

The warmth that I feel is like the sun all around

It places a desire to search for more,

And it all begins with a door.

Here I am! I stand at the door and knock.

If anyone hears my voice and opens the door,

I will come in and eat with that person, and they with me.

Revelation 3:20 NIV

FORGIVENESS

Forgiveness is an action that can transform those who choose it.

Forgiveness is an attitude to see others from another point of view.

Forgiveness is a fountain whose source is not my own.

Forgiveness is freedom from anger, bitterness, and revenge.

Forgiveness is a balm from life's assaults and pains.

Forgiveness is peace for the chaos and hurt.

Forgiveness is hope for our heart's restoration.

Forgiveness is a foundation to begin anew.

Forgiveness is a purifier for a weary troubled heart.

Forgiveness is an open door that welcomes an old friend.

Forgiveness is a teacher that shows us our nature.

Forgiveness is a mirror that reflects my own needs.

Forgiveness is the antidote for the poison of abuse.

Forgiveness is powerful to break the chains of regret.

Forgiveness is the release from the heavy burdens we carry.

Forgiveness is the answer for healing the troubled soul.

Forgiveness is the pathway to peace within.

Forgiveness can bring healing to the pain of strife.

Forgiveness is the gift that was first given to me.

Forgiveness is meant to be shared not to withhold.

Forgiveness is a place that was paid for at the cross.

Forgiveness is to surrender the offense to the Holy Judge.

Be kind to one another, tenderhearted, forgiving one another,

as God in Christ forgave you.

Ephesians 4:32 ESV

IRISH BLESSING

May the twinkle in your eyes never fade

as you draws close to each other,

May the sun's light shine bright

on the path that you walk together.

May you kneel often in prayer,

and listen for His words for guidance.

May the presence of the Lord fill your home

and you experience the peace that He brings.

May you feel the strength of your bond

each time you hold hands.

Remember why you fell in love

When frustration and conflicts arise.

When the storms of life come,

may you shelter each other.

May laughter be heard

from the windows of your home.

May each morning bring new joy

for the hope it brings.

May the dreams of your hearts

be realized through the work of your hands.

May your bedroom be a place of peace and passion.

And when the autumn of life comes,

May together you look back over your journey,

To see the beauty of your life together.

THE PARTY

Her steps were light as she crept down the hall,

She had to see just a glimpse of the ball.

Music and laughter told of the way,

The guests had arrived, and the mood was gay.

She stayed hidden and careful not to make a sound,

Her movement cautious, not to be found.

Carefully observing the incredible sight,

Knowing that the party was just tonight.

The sparkle and glamour of gowns and dresses,

Expensive jewelry and beautiful tresses,

Men in suits that fit like gloves,

Shirts white as the wings of doves.

The sound of voices in important conversations,

People had come from many destinations.

Her eyes moved from person to person straining to see,

If her love would be there, was the heart's plea.

Her love was unknown to the man that she seeks,

She promised herself -- only a few peeks.

She spun around at the sound of his voice,

Her heart fluttered in excitement as if to rejoice.

She carefully withdrew to a place to observe,

Back by the curtains along the wall with a curve.

She could see her love as he spoke with ease,

All listened to him knowing of his expertise.

Lost for a moment, she forgot the time,

Until the sound of the clock with its loud chime.

She must leave holding this sight in her heart,

Her love was so naive and pure from the start.

She returned to her place with the forgotten,

She stood folding the linens made with fine cotton.

Reliving the sights and memories of the night,

Her eyes twinkled and shone with delight.

He is educated and respected.

His sincere kindness is unexpected.

Her heart filled with an overflow of emotion,

But he is unaware of her work or devotion.

Her work seems lighter as her fantasy grows,

Dreaming of when her fragrance is of a rose.

Her dress of silk fabric and fine style,

When he takes her hand with a soft smile.

One day her heart says, "I will know of his embrace,

We will dance the waltz with ease and grace.

Moving to the music, lost in the atmosphere,

To hear the sound of his whispers in my ear."

A smile flashed across the beautiful young face,

She felt the flush of color as her heart did race.

Glancing quickly to check if anyone had seen,

Oh, the matron is watching, her eyes so keen.

Late into the night before the work was complete,

Her exit of the mansion to the empty dark street.

Her steps deliberate to reach home before dawn,

No lamp lights, no taxis, the people were all gone.

Her thoughts took her to the hours before,

In the room again wanting to experience more.

Lost in remembering she didn't see the horse,

As it galloped towards her with its great force.

A shout from the rider startled her, she screamed,

The rider pulled the horse to a stop, he too was startled, it seemed.

"What are you doing out at this hour?" he said,

"I am returning home from work," she said, lowering her head.

In utter surprise, she knew the voice in the dark,

"It is not wise to be out, at this time of the night," his remark.

She shuttered then said weakly, "thank you sir, I will be all right,"

"I insist to see you home, since I gave you such a fright."

He raised her to the saddle with one swift lift,

Oblivious of her love in this incredible gift.

She sat in astonishment as he held on to her,

As the horse carried them, she felt safe and secure.

Her voice in whisper to tell him which door,

At once, he could see that she is of a family so poor.

Without a word, he jumped from the fine steed,

His hands gently lowered her, his final kind deed.

She blushed as she tried to speak,

He leaned in smiling, then kissed her cheek.

"Please take more care as you walk home so late.

Many dangers and thieves lie in wait."

"Thank you, sir, you have been most courteous",

His broad smile and a wink in a manner chivalrous,

In one quick move he is back on the horse,

He galloped away returning to his course.

Her hands trembled as she grasped the handle,

The room was dark as she searched for the candle.

Sleep won't come easy for me tonight,

My heart's too full, it's overcome with delight.

She sat writing by the candles' soft glow,

She knew, no one would ever know.

Nevertheless, for her this night would never fade,

For a brief moment, she was not a mere maid.

FOGGY MORNINGS

As a soft light shines on the horizon,

The sky is grey and hazy.

Even though I can't see the sun today,

I know it is there.

The fog has covered the sun's brightness,

Yet I know the sun is still there shining brightly.

Many times in my life the trials and problems

Have blocked my view of the Son,

Yet He is still there! His word tells me,

He will never leave me or forsake me.

His word also says NOTHING,

Can separate me from His love.

His power is not diminished because I can't see Him!

He is the same yesterday, today, and forever,

Praise the Lord for His faithfulness.

Even though, at times I may not see Him working,

I am confident, that He is at work.

Foggy mornings remind me: God is always with me.

... "Teaching them to observe all things

that I have commanded you;

and lo, I am with you always, even to the end of the age." Amen.

Jesus said in Matthew 28:20 NKJV

THE VALLEY OF WAIT

The doctor calls the family to say all has been done,

The time has come to enter the valley of the wait.

The journey begins with listening for the call of The Son,

To lay aside the earthly and move toward the heavenly gate.

Friends and family gather to reminisce and to share,

Caring words are spoken to all there.

Stories are shared often with a tear,

Then a gentle "I love you" whispered in the ear.

Voices speak of the days in their life,

The path that was filled with love, joy and some strife.

Time passes slowly in the valley of the wait,

It is hard on family and friends of this date.

It's sad to say a fond goodbye to life here below,

But having the joy of them being in heaven's glow.

Music and songs played gently around,

Lightening the mood, we have found.

We remind them of the home that is waiting,

A special place that Jesus himself is creating.

In the valley, the ebb and flow of emotions are present,

Brings to the surface the conflict of joy and lament.

We watch with love in the transition,

While heaven awaits the precious addition.

Soon to be released into the Father's embrace,

Then to see the Savior face to face.

In the eternal heavenly land of pure light,

Mother, father and others are there to see the first delight.

There is a message in the valley, it is a promise of hope,

That is the foundation for us to face this and to cope.

The time in the Valley of the Wait will conclude,

We will join them someday with hearts of gratitude.

Let not your heart be troubled:

ye believe in God, believe also in me.

In my Father's house are many mansions:

if it were not so, I would have told you.

I go to prepare a place for you.

And if I go and prepare a place for you,

I will come again, and receive you unto myself;

that where I am, there ye may be also.

And whither I go ye know, and the way ye know.

John 14:1-4 KJV

THE NAMELESS

There are so many nameless people in the Bible. Yet each one is part of God's story: The woman at the well, the man lowered through the roof, the boy Elijah healed, the woman with the oil and many more.

They are people like you and me. People who trusted God in the midst of a crisis or who quietly served. Remember the widow and her mites? A boy who gave his lunch to the disciples?

Not one of them were unknown, nor nameless to God our Heavenly Father. His word tells us that He has engraved our names on the palms of His hands. He knows my name.

"To me that is comforting to know, I hope it is for you.

See, I have engraved you on the palms of my hands;"

Isaiah 49:16a NIV

THE UNSEEN WARRIOR

You might not see the unseen warrior who has set sleep aside for a more urgent need.

The Father's book lays open to the warrior, as the lamp gives light. The warrior shares the burden with His faithful friend, who listens through the long quiet hours.

As the war rages, complete destruction looms on the horizon. Yet the unseen warrior continues to battle for those caught in the conflict.

The warrior has seen these battles before, knowing that there is much at stake. The lives of those in the battle are so important to the warrior, not wanting anyone to be hurt or be lost.

The unseen warrior can be seen on bended knee, pulling the weeds in a garden and talking to the One that is always present. Each weed becomes a formed prayer seeking answers to the problems in the warrior's heart. There is gentle care to protect the growing harvest during the time of pulling the weeds. As the warrior works through the field, the peace grows as pulled weeds pile up.

In an old rocking chair, you might see the warrior rock, the eyes might be closed yet you see the lips moving silently. Time passes without measure, as the words of love are recalled from the Father's book. More time in prayer is spent as tears flow freely. Whispers continue in the voiceless battle.

You can see the warrior in the old church at the altar, surrendering the war to the only One that knows the end from the beginning. The warrior is confident that all of the prayers fill the bowls of sweet incense in the presence of the eternal Father. The warrior is certain the prayers will never fade nor will they expire. There is an assurance that the Loving Father will answer each prayer according to His will.

At times unseen warriors have grown weary and felt wounded and worn. The loving Father reminds the warrior that their time in the battle has not been in vain, those prayers have made a difference in many loved one's lives and in the heavenly realm. Even though the warrior may not know the results of the prayers until the warrior stands at the heavenly throne, the battle continues to be waged through fervent prayer.

To all the unseen warriors, please don't give up the fight. When you feel like it is too much, run to the Savior, whose blood paid the price for our sins and our eternal life.

Refresh your spirit at the fountain of living water.

Oh, weary warrior, stay at the spring to renew your strength and passion to stay in the fight. Let the Holy Spirit renew and replenish your spirit to be ready for the next battle that you are called to.

Confess your faults one to another,

and pray one for another, that ye may be healed.

The effectual fervent prayer of a righteous man availeth much.

James 5:16 KJV

WHEN YOU BROKE IN

I don't know when you broke in.

Your very presence poisoned me.

You worked in secret trying to take hold of me.

You have tried to disrupt my life. You have upset my family.

You have thrown uncertainty and fear at me.

Let me tell you this: You have been discovered!

I will do everything within my power to destroy you!

Even though you attack my body, you can't touch

what makes me who I am.

You can't steal my spirit, I know my strength comes from on high.

I know I will not walk this path alone, many others cheer me on.

I set my sights on healing and wholeness.

You will not win!

A Year

It surprised her today, it has been nearly a year,

The painful truths that made it unbearably clear.

Dreadful signs led to the only real choice,

"This is not life, nor is it love" said her heart's voice.

She had hoped, she had prayed,

A different outcome began to fade.

She had made countless pleas,

With her life on her knees.

Packing up a life with all its dreams,

Trying to quiet her heart as it screams.

Tears flowed freely as she took one last look,

As to close this chapter in her life's book.

Her hands shook as she found her keys,

Doubt spoke loudly to sway and to tease.

A new life to begin she knows not what,

She paused at the door then pulled it shut.

She began the drive to a safe place,

The stains of the tears marked her face.

A call came from miles away,

The caller spoke truth as she made her way.

Fresh hope, new goals and dreams to believe,

The hurt, pain and deception will leave.

Time to heal, restore and to rest,

To know that with Christ she is blessed.

Nearly a year has passed how could it be?

She lived through the pain and is able to see.

That day was a start and not the end,

Her life is more whole, she is on the mend.

The healing and comfort is hard to explain,

The balm of His peace applied on her pain.

The questions, the doubts, and fears are just

To remember His love is to trust.

JUST ONE CALL CAN HELP US...

To know we need God.

To see we are helpless.

To know we alone can't fix it.

To know that life is fragile.

To find an old friend.

To say our last good-bye.

To hear of a miracle.

To bind up a heart's wound.

To see God's provision.

To mend a relationship.

To be a special blessing.

To offer a needed prayer.

To offer grace to someone.

To bring peace to a desperate soul.

TIME

Me time

Family time

Wait Time

Overtime

Personal time

Short time

Last time

Play time

Time is at hand

Time on our hands

Start time

Time waits for no man

Practice time

Another time

Give me time

Timeless

A matter of time

No time

Time heals

Wasting time

Now is the time

Peace time

Half Time

End Time

Time is money

Time out

Time stands still

Time flies

Quitting time

Time is up

Next time

Make time count

Why, you do not even know what will happen tomorrow.
What is your life? You are a mist that appears for a little while
and then vanishes.

James 4:14 NIV

DREAMS

Buried beneath the rubble of disappointments,
Abandoned along the road of events.
Forgotten and faded like an old sketch,
Too tired to believe, to reach and stretch.

Where did they go, when were they lost?
Was it too hard or too high the cost?
When did the dream get tossed aside?
When was it that the dreams died?

Dreams of innocent thoughts and desires,
Of wishes and hopes to come, it requires.
Dreams of what could be and what should be,
To believe in the dream is the key.

Dreams help to move us beyond the past,

To dream is to take us to places so vast.

They show that life is full of new starts,

New loves, desires and hopes for the hearts.

Dreams push us to think outside of the box,

They cause us to see a path, not just the rocks.

Dreams stretch and pull us to believe in possibilities,

To a realm that only an open heart sees.

Dreams reach beyond our limitations,

They can be found in our imaginations.

Dreams transport us to new unknown destinations,

They are our new desires and fascinations.

Dreams live in the realm of possibilities,

Dreams have visions that only know abilities.

Planted by the Creator made for each,

It is a tool by Him to cause us to reach.

Dreams are watered by faith each day,

And wrapped tightly to keep doubt at bay.

Dreams begin from a seed planted long ago,

So deep it begins and then to reality to grow.

They're remembered in the times we pray,

Each step with the dream brings us closer each day.

Closer to know what is the Father's vision,

And to know His plans are made with precision.

Dreams teach us to see past the doubt and fear,

Hopelessness and sadness will disappear.

When the dreams begin to take shape,

Then their reality is our landscape.

Dreams show us our courage and strength,

So, see the journey and the great length.

Of our Creator's love and design,

That His dreams are pure and divine.

His plans and ideas are like a kaleidoscope,

His dreams bring life, love and hope.

They bring a refreshing new vision.

To take hold of the dream is our decision.

GIVE BACK MY HEART

You said the love died, something you tried to hide.

No sense in pretending, the hurt is too deep for mending.

How did it occur? You don't know? Maybe, it happened so slow.

We were too busy to see, now you want to be free.

So I say, go on your way, a new life I'll start.

But, give back my heart, it is not yours anymore.

I'll be fine you will see, because, I too have been set free!

Do You Hear Him

Do you hear Him as you read His book?

When over your life's journey you look?

Is it when you worship and sing,

Or when a hurting heart you bring?

As you stand at a sink with dirty dishes,

While telling Him your unspoken wishes?

Do you hear His gentle voice?

In a struggle with a difficult choice?

Do you hear Him speak through His word?

While welling tears make the pages blurred?

In moments of peace in a quiet place,

Knowing it is only Jesus who gives eternal grace?

Do you hear His voice during life's sorrow?

Or wondering what will happen tomorrow?

Does His voice speak tenderly through life's trials?

As He holds firmly to your hand all the while.

Do you hear Him tell you of His abiding love?

And feel His presence pour over you from above?

Do you hear His voice give guidance and direction?

That comes from His great heart of compassion?

In the midst of life when you stumble and fall,

Even there, have you heard Him when He calls?

Have you heard His invitation to the cross of salvation?

The place of forgiveness, healing and restoration.

"Come to me, my child, I know your heart"

He says softly, "All the hurts, pain, every part."

Do you hear Him say, "That's too heavy, it's too much?"

"I will help you; the load is light with my touch."

He calls to us in the brightness of the day,

Through all our activities of work and play.

He calls in the dark silence and loneliness of night,

While we wonder and imagine tomorrow's fight.

Do you hear His voice to come to a place of peace?

Only there is where the burdens will be released.

He calls us to remain so very near,

He says, "Come to me, do not fear."

In the midst of life's hardships and crashes,

Listen to His voice tell us, "I bring beauty from ashes."

NOTES

I am often asked, "What inspired you to write that?" So, I am including a note of the inspiration for each of the writings in "*When My Heart Sings*."

— **Brenda Carroll Jarvis**

THE CLOCK — As I reflected on how I was growing older, I realized that more time was behind me than is ahead of me. I remembered that God holds time in his hand.

AN ENEMY LURKS NEARBY—This was inspired when I watched a news report. My heart grew heavy seeing the hatred displayed.

WEARY FEET — I often think of Jesus walking the dusty roads from town to town. I thought of his tired feet, dusty and calloused. Those weary feet brought us the news that Salvation had come.

SO, WHAT IS NEW? — Inspired by a conversation I heard. A person asked "So, what is new?" We have many opportunities to share our faith and so many need to hear of Jesus and Salvation.

HOLD MY HAND — This poem was written during the time in my life when I was adjusting to being divorced and asking the Lord how to navigate through unfamiliar pathways.

WHAT I HEAR — Was inspired by Revelation 3:20 "Here I am! I stand at the door and knock. If anyone hears my voice and opens the door, I will come in and eat with him, and he with me."

FORGIVENESS — I woke with the word forgiveness on my mind, I felt an urgency to pray and write. The words flowed as I saw in my mind the power that forgiveness has.

THE PARTY — Was written when I was recently divorced. I wanted to write of how a girl might dream.

FOGGY MORNINGS — One morning the fog was low and heavy. The fog obscured the sunrise, but I never doubted that the sun was there.

THE UNSEEN WARRIOR — This expresses the battle that rages around us. I am a person who prays, and I know that many times I have sensed the need to pray for people who are going through difficult times.

THE NAMELESS — So many people in the Bible are not named, but their lives and experiences are written for us to see God's great love and mercy.

THE VALLEY OF WAIT — As my mother was nearing the end of her time here on earth, this was the expression of my heart.

WHEN YOU BROKE IN — Written when I was diagnosed with breast cancer. It was a declaration of God being in charge, not anything else.

A YEAR — I wrote this a year after my divorce. It was a testimony to the healing hand of the Lord.

WE ARE JUST ONE CALL AWAY FROM — This was inspired by how communication brings all kinds of information and how we can share Jesus in every situation.

MAKE TIME COUNT — Time drives our society, but do we make time count?

DREAMS — This was written as a way to sort out emotions while adjusting to a new life after my divorce.

GIVE BACK MY HEART — Was inspired when I chose to move forward after my divorce.

THE GIFT OF SUNRISE — Was inspired by Psalms 143:8 NIV "Let the morning bring me word of your unfailing love, for I have put my trust in you. Show me the way I should go, for to you I entrust my life."

ABOUT THE AUTHOR

BRENDA CARROL JARVIS is a very active Christian woman. She was a missionary in Mexico City for 17 years and after returning to the United States she started a music ministry and performed many concerts with some of the biggest names in Southern Gospel Music.

Brenda is a frequent speaker for Christian women's events. She does portrayals of Biblical women when requested. She maintains two websites: *goldenstreetsingers.com*, for her music ministry, *Brendavotions.com,* where she posts her devotional writings and her poetry.

She has written and published three books, *Biblical Women of Influence*, *It Happened in Bethlehem* and *When My Heart Sings*. All are available from her website, *Brendavotions.com*. She has completed her next book to be published this year, *Hope for All of Us.*

Brenda enjoys sharing her faith wherever the Lord leads her. Often, she will pray with or encourage people via telephone. It is Brenda's passion that everyone understands the great gift in salvation, the power of God's unlimited love and the transformational grace through Jesus Christ.

Brenda is a frequent speaker for Christian women's events. She does portrayals of Biblical women when requested. She maintains two websites: *goldenstreetsingers.com*, for her music ministry, and *Brendavotions.com,* where she posts her devotional writings and her poetry.

She grew up in Fort Wayne, IN, but now resides in the summers in a Civil War-era farmhouse in Farmdale, OH, and the winters in a coastal-area cottage in Brunswick, GA.